From The Abby Aldrich Rockefeller Folk Art Center
Williamsburg, Virginia

The Folk Art Counting Book

Based on a Concept Originated by Florence Cassen Mayers

Developed by Amy Watson and the Staff of
The Abby Aldrich Rockefeller Folk Art Center

The Colonial Williamsburg Foundation
Williamsburg, Virginia

In association with

Harry N. Abrams, Inc., Publishers, New York

© 1992 by
The Colonial Williamsburg Foundation

Published in 1992 by
The Colonial Williamsburg Foundation, Williamsburg,
Virginia, and Harry N. Abrams, Incorporated, New York,
a Times Mirror Company

The Folk Art Counting Book is based on a concept by
Florence Cassen Mayers, the author of nine ABC Museum
Books published by Harry N. Abrams, Inc.

Special thanks to Anne Watkins and the staff of the Abby
Aldrich Rockefeller Folk Art Center for their assistance

ISBN 0-87935-084-9 (C. W.)
ISBN 0-8109-3306-3 (Abrams)

Printed in Hong Kong

This book was designed by Helen Mageras

Cover: *Noah's Ark*, attributed to Joseph Henry Hidley, Poestenkill, N. Y.,
ca. 1870, oil on wood panel, 57.101.8

Title Page: *Yellowlegs (Feeder)*, maker unidentified, America, ca. 1900,
carved and painted wood, 67.702.1; *Black-Necked Stilt*, maker unidentified,
probably Massachusetts or New York, possibly 1900–1914, carved and
painted wood with cord-wrapped nail for beak, 57.702.6

olk art is the product of untrained artists who, although unfamiliar with the rules for rendering correct linear perspective, anatomy, or color balance or the proper use of light and shadow, somehow solve the technical difficulties they encounter and intuitively produce satisfying pictures, carvings, and household furnishings. The images in *The Folk Art Counting Book* are from the extensive eighteenth-, nineteenth-, and twentieth-century collection of American folk art at the Abby Aldrich Rockefeller Folk Art Center in Williamsburg, Virginia, one of the country's premier collections.

Abby Aldrich Rockefeller's appreciation for folk art's aesthetic appeal led her to collect over six hundred pieces in the late 1920s and 1930s. In 1939 she presented the principal part of this collection to the Colonial Williamsburg Foundation. It is the nucleus of the Abby Aldrich Rockefeller Folk Art Center, which was built in her memory by her husband, John D. Rockefeller, Jr., and opened in 1957. The present collection numbers more than 2,600 objects and continues to grow through gifts and purchases.

The Folk Art Counting Book is designed for young learners but it will be enjoyed by all ages. Small children can start at one whirligig and soon learn to count up to five weather vanes, ten jungle animals, and twenty eagles. The uncluttered pages with large, clear numbers that are immediately recognizable in a repetitive quilt border make this book easy to use as a learning tool. Outstanding examples of folk art such as the endearing *Baby in Red Chair*, the wooden animals whittled by itinerant carver Wilhelm Schimmel, and Henry Church's *The Monkey Picture* have been specially selected to enhance young children's appreciation of folk art and to stimulate their visual and cognitive senses.

Sit together and help your child learn to count all nineteen members of *The Quilting Party*. Or encourage children to explore the charm of folk art on their own.

A descriptive listing of the objects illustrated appears at the back of the book.

Count 1 whirligig

Count 1 baby

Count 2 children

Count 2 eyes

Count 3 horses

How many men?
How many swords?

Count 4 wooden men

4

Count 4 cats playing

5

Count 5 weather vanes

Count 6 birds

Count 6 shoes

How many boots?

7

Count 8 dogs

Count 9 windows in the house

Count 9 green leaves

Count 10 jungle animals

Count 11 Easter eggs

Count 12 people

Count 13 animals

How many children?

14

Count 14 train wheels
How many passengers?

Count 15 hearts

Count 15 sails

16

Count 16 Indians

Danse Militaire des Sauvages devant Le President T. Monroe. 1821

Count 16 diamonds
How many circles?

Count 17 stars

18

Count 18 buttons

Count 19 people

Count 20 lions

Count 20 eagles

When more than one object appears on a page, the identification is from left to right.

1. *Military Man*, maker unidentified, America, possibly 1860–1880, carved and painted wood, 79.700.2; *Baby in Red Chair*, artist unidentified, possibly Pennsylvania, ca. 1810–1830, oil on canvas, 31.100.1

2. *Spectacles*, attributed to E. G. Washburne & Co., New York, N. Y., 1875–1910, painted zinc, 57.806.1; *Children with Toys*, attributed to Sturtevant J. Hamblin, probably Massachusetts, ca. 1845, oil on canvas, 57.100.5; *The Monkey Picture*, Henry Church, Chagrin Falls, Ohio, 1895–1900, oil on paper mounted on canvas, 81.103.1

3. *Three Horsemen*, artist unidentified, probably Pennsylvania, dated March 1849, watercolor and ink on paper, 58.305.8

4. *Politician*, maker unidentified, America, 1875–1900, carved and painted wood and leather, 63.705.1; *Santa Claus*, attributed to Charles Robb, probably New York, N. Y., 1875–1900, carved and painted wood, 61.705.1; *Officer*, maker unidentified, America, probably 1875–1890, carved and painted wood and metal, 57.705.2; *Naval Officer*, maker unidentified, possibly late eighteenth century, polychromed white pine, 57.705.1; *Four Cats Playing*, artist unidentified, America, probably 1846–1865, watercolor and pencil on wove paper, 58.301.10

5. *Horse*, maker unidentified, America, 1870–1890, gilded copper and lead, 66.800.4; *Running Deer*, maker unidentified, possibly Quakertown, Pa., possibly 1890–1910, sheet and bar iron, 31.800.5; *Butterfly*, maker unidentified, 1875–1900, painted copper, 62.800.2; *Rooster*, maker unidentified, America, 1850–1875, painted sheet copper, 72.800.2; *Cheviot Sheep*, maker unidentified, America, probably 1875–1900, copper and zinc with gilt, 32.800.6

6. *Crib Quilt*, attributed to Alma Richter, Sunman, Ripley Co., Ind., probably 1854, various cottons, 85.609.1; *Josiah Turner Boot Sign*, artist unidentified, probably Massachusetts, ca. 1810, oil on white pine, 58.707.1

7. *Tiger*, 60.701.3; *Eagle*, 70.701.6; *Lion*, 63.701.4; *Owl*, 62.701.6; *Parrot*, 59.701.4; *Eagle*, 32.701.3; *Spotted Dog*, 70.701.7. Carvings attributed to Wilhelm Schimmel, Pennsylvania, mid- to late nineteenth century, carved and painted pine

8. *Eskimo Dogs*, Justin McCarthy, America, 1960, oil on board, 71.101.1

9. *The Yellow Coach*, artist unidentified, America, probably 1815–1835, oil on canvas, 32.101.3; *Album Quilt* (detail), maker unidentified, America, probably ca. 1850, various cottons with some silk details, 85.609.5

10. *Dark Jungle*, Victor Joseph Gatto, probably New York, N. Y., ca. 1950, oil on canvas, 73.101.1

11. *Easter Rabbit*, attributed to John Conrad Gilbert, Berks (now Schuylkill) Co., Pa., probably 1795–1800, watercolor and ink on laid paper, 59.305.3

12. *The Old Plantation*, artist unidentified, probably South Carolina, possibly 1790–1800, watercolor on laid paper, 35.301.3

13. *The Peaceable Kingdom*, Edward Hicks, Bucks Co., Pa., 1832–1834, oil on canvas, 32.101.1

14. *Miner's Train*, Jack Savitsky, Pennsylvania, 1970, enamel on plywood, 71.110.1

15. *Putman Family Record*, John T. Adams, possibly New York State, 1844, watercolor and ink on wove paper, 57.305.1; *Ship with Paper Border*, artist unidentified, America, 1805–1825, oil on canvas with block-printed paper border, 58.111.3

16. *Indian War Dance*, attributed to the Baroness Hyde de Neuville, Washington, D. C., 1821, watercolor, pencil, and ink on laid paper, 31.301.9; *Quilt Square—Rollins Family Record*, probably Ebenezer and Betsey Rollins, New Hampshire, ca. 1840, cotton, 62.609.1

17. *Birth and Baptismal Certificate for Elias Hamman*, attributed to the Strasburg Artist, Shenandoah Co., Va., possibly 1806, watercolor, gouache, and ink on wove paper, 81.305.1

18. *Ezra Weston, Jr.*, attributed to Rufus Hathaway, probably Duxbury, Mass., probably 1793, oil on canvas, 72.100.2

19. *The Quilting Party*, artist unidentified, America, probably 1854–1875, oil and pencil on paper adhered to plywood, 37.101.1

20. *Coverlet*, B. French, Waterville, N. Y., dated 1835, blue wool and white cotton, double cloth weave, 73.609.9; *Double-Woven Coverlet*, James Alexander, near New Britain, N. Y., 1822, dark blue wool with white cotton, 78.609.5